Leaving The Past Behind

Copyright 2024
By Karen Dowling

Dedication

I would like to dedicate this book to my best friend in this world and to my lifetime love...Tom Watt.

Thank you for seeing who I am and for always believing in me.

Contents:

- **Acknowledgments**

- **Chapter One- We all have a past**

- **Chapter Two- A man named Job**

- **Chapter Three- A man named Joseph**

- Chapter Four- A man named Saul

- Chapter Five- My Story

- Chapter Six- Final Thoughts

Acknowledgments:

Without the Lord, this book would never have been written. He freed me from a life of sin, of pain, of shame, failure, and darkness. He brought me into a life of freedom, of joy, of peace, happiness, and success in doing what I love. I will spend forever thanking Him. He is my everything.

Chapter One: We all have a Past

Memories. They can be one of the most

valuable treasures that we possess in this life,

that is- unless the memories are not good ones. That is when they can become one of the biggest obstacles to our well-being, growth, and to a successful future. There is probably not a single person living that does not have any bad memories from their past. Most of the time a few bad memories do not have the power to keep us from moving forward in our life, but when the bad memories are so horrific that they haunt us, or there are too many of them to get past then those memories have the power to destroy our well-being and our future.

Let me assure you that no matter how alone, how hurt, how angry, or ashamed you might feel over the past- you are not alone. Every single person that has lived any length of time has some bad memories of their own. One of Satan's great ploys is to isolate us and then to make us feel like no one has been as awful as we are. Or he tells us that no one could ever understand the pain we have suffered, or how deep and unbearable it is. That is simply not true!

Let me tell you a story about a man in the bible named Job.

Chapter Two: A man named Job

Job lived in the early days and we can find him in the book of Job. Many people go through their lives believing that no one could ever understand their pain, or that no one has suffered as unjustly as they have, but that simply is not true. Many people have suffered tragic circumstances that they feel they did not deserve and do not have the answers as to why. Bad things often happen to good people, mostly because we live in a fallen world that is filled with wickedness and innocent people are some of it's victims everyday. The real question though is not **WHY** it happened as much as it is **HOW** we will respond to it, because the answer to this question will determine what your future will look like.

Let me share a story with you about a man named Job that went through tremendous loss, suffering, and pain. In the first chapter of the book of Job it tells us a story of a man that lived in the land of Uz, whose name was Job (Job 1:1). It also states that Job was **BLAMELESS** and **UPRIGHT** and one who **FEARED GOD** and **SHUNNED EVIL**. Job had done nothing deserving of all the calamity that befell him.

So further down in the chapter it states that there came a day when the sons of God (Angels) came before the Lord on an appointed day to present themselves before God, and Satan also came to present himself. When he came God asked him where he had come from, to which he replied "From going to and fro upon the earth, and from walking back and forth on it" (Job 1:6,7). So God asked him if he had noticed His servant Job and seen what a good man he was, to which

Satan replied that the only reason Job loved God was because God had put a hedge of protection around him, his household, and all that he owned.

Satan then challenges God by saying that if He removed the protection from around him and all that Job possessed then Job would curse God to His face. In other words, Satan was saying that Job would only love God when things were going his way. How many times is that not true of us? When life is good and pleasant we love God, but when things are not going our way we either get angry with God or feel that God is angry with us or does not love us.

God then allows Satan to touch Job and all that he has, only he is forbidden from taking his life. So Satan then runs around with his new found freedom. The day soon came when Job's sons and daughters were feasting in their eldest brother's house as they routinely did and a messenger came to deliver the news to Job that the Sabeans (South Arabians) had raided his land and taken all of his oxen and all of his donkeys. Thousands of livestock gone in one day and killed all of his servants tending to them. At the same time, while the servant was still speaking, another of Job's servants came running up to tell him that hailstones of fire had fallen down from heaven and killed all of his sheep and the servants tending them had been killed with the edge of the sword. Again, thousands of livestock gone in a moment.

While this servant was still speaking yet another servant came to tell Job that the Chaldeans (later became the Babylonians) had raided and stolen all the camels (hundreds) and killed the servants tending them with the edge of the sword. While this servant was still speaking another came to tell Job that while his grown sons and daughters were feasting in their eldest brother's house, a strong wind came from across the wilderness knocking the entire house down on his children, killing all of them (Job 1:13-19).

Then Job rose up, tore his robe, and shaved his head and he fell to the ground and bowed down in reverence to the Lord stating these words, "Naked I came from my mother's womb and naked I shall return there. The Lord gave and the Lord has taken away. Blessed be the name of the Lord". In all this Job did not sin nor charge God with any wrong (Job 1:20-22). Obviously Job had quite a bit of possessions. In fact, the book of Job states that he was the greatest of ALL people in the East and was rich, highly respected, and famous in his homeland. So you can be sure that there was lots of talking and speculating about what had happened to Job and WHY this was happening to him. As we will discover further into this book, Job also had many of his own questions for God.

Beginning with Chapter Two of the book of Job, `we read that Satan has another conversation with God in which God states, "Have you considered my servant Job, that there is none like him on the earth, a blameless and upright man, one who fears God and shuns evil? And still he holds fast to his integrity, although YOU INCITED ME AGAINST HIM TO DESTROY HIM WITHOUT CAUSE (Job 2:3)! Satan responds to God with these words, "Skin for skin! Yes, all that a man has he will give for his life. But stretch out Your hand now and touch his bone and his flesh and he will surely curse You to Your face" (Job

2:4,5)! God then replies, "Behold, he is in your hand, but spare his life (Job 2:6).

So, as we can see, Job's trial comes from a conversation between God and Satan, in which Satan is basically saying that Job only loves God because nothing bad has befallen him. God however, knows differently, for He knows what is in every heart. So as our story of Job continues, we see next that Satan strikes Job with painful boils from the soles of his feet to the crown of his head, and Job takes a potsherd and scrapes himself as he sits in the midst of ashes (Job 2:7).

Then Job's wife approaches him and says, "Do you still hold fast to your integrity? Curse God and die" (Job 2:9)! Then Job replies, "You speak as one of the foolish women speak. Shall we indeed accept GOOD from God, and **SHALL WE NOT ACCEPT ADVERSITY**"? In all this Job **DID NOT SIN WITH HIS LIPS** (Job 2:10).

After this, three of Jobs closest friends, hearing of all his adversity that had come upon him, came to console him and when they saw him from far off and did not recognize him, they began to cry out, weep, tear their robes in grief, and throw ashes upon their heads as was the custom for mourning. They sat down on the ground for seven days and seven nights and no one spoke a word to him because they perceived that Job's grief was **VERY GREAT**. The next thirty four chapters of Job are filled with Job's three friends trying to convince Job that he must have done SOMETHING to deserve all the calamity that had befallen him, and Job responding by defending his own innocence.

Have you ever been in a similar situation where the well-meaning people around you are actually making your suffering worse? Well this was Job's situation. Finally, as Job is crying out to God for understanding for answers as to why this has happened to him, God answered. He then has a conversation with Job that changes everything. He reveals himself to Job in a way that heals him, restores him, strengthens him, and renews him. At the end of their conversation Job makes a statement that reveals this. He says, "I have heard of You by the hearing of the ear, but now my eye SEES YOU" (Job 42:5).

You see, it only takes one encounter with the living God for everything to change. As we also discover at the end of the book of Job, "The Lord BLESSED the latter days of Job MORE than his beginning, for he had fourteen thousand sheep, six thousand camels, one thousand yoke of oxen, and one thousand female donkeys. He also had seven sons and three daughters. And he called the name of the first one Jemimah, the name of the second one Keziah, and the name of the third one Keren-Happuch. In all the land were found no women so beautiful as the daughters of Job, and their father gave them an inheritance among their brothers" (Job 42: 12-15).

God actually doubled everything that Job possessed. One interesting fact about this is something my children once asked me about when I read the story of Job to them many years ago. I went down the line with everything Job originally possessed and how God doubled it. In the beginning of the book of Job we read that Job possessed 7,000 sheep and then God doubled it to 14,000. He had 3,000 camels and God doubled it to 6,000. He owned 500 yoke of oxen and God doubled it to 1,000. He had 500 female donkeys and God doubled it to 1,000. He also had 7 sons and 3 daughters which God replaced with 7 sons and 3 daughters. One of my daughters immediately spoke up and said that God did NOT double EVERYTHING because He gave Job the same amount of sons and daughters that he had before. It was a very important observation and one that the Holy Spirit immediately revealed to me WHY. This revelation also puts to rest the question asked by almost all people everywhere...is there life after death? Is our soul eternal? The answer to that question is a resounding YES! It is answered in the book of Job. You see, God DID double everything Job possessed, INCLUDING HIS CHILDREN. His first 10 children were STILL ALIVE, but living in Heaven with God. Job had 10 children LIVING in Heaven and 10 children living on earth!

The main point of this story about Job is this…Job's pain and suffering was the result of his faith in God and his love for God being tested. God never tempts us or entices us to sin. Temptation comes when we are enticed by our own lusts and desires, and then pulled away from God by them. However, God DOES test His people to reveal their hearts. There are many possible reasons we experience adversity, suffering, or pain. Testing is only one of them. Let me tell you of another person in the bible who experienced his own share of pain and suffering. It was young man by the name of Joseph.

Chapter Three: A Man Named Joseph

In the book of Genesis, there was a man named Jacob who had twelve sons. Ten of his sons were born to him by his wife Leah. Two of his sons were born to him by his wife Rachael. Jacob loved Rachael more than Leah. The fact was that the only reason Jacob had Leah as a wife was because he was tricked into marrying her by his uncle Laban.

Jacob loved Rachael from the moment he first laid eyes on her, so he asked his uncle Laban for her hand in marriage. Laban agreed, but only if Jacob would work for him as his servant for seven years, and after that he would give Rachael to Jacob as his wife. Jacob quickly agreed and it was said that "Jacob served seven years for Rachael, and it only seemed a few days to him because of the love he had for Rachael (Genesis 29:20)".

Seven years passed by quickly for Jacob and now it was time for him to receive from Laban what he had worked so hard for- Rachael. The wedding day came and Jacob was wed to his bride, but when Jacob went into the tent to consummate his marriage to Rachael, he lifted her wedding veil only to find Leah!

Understandably, he was furious and when he approached Laban about this deception, Laban replied that it was not his people's custom to give the younger daughter in marriage before the older daughter.

He told Jacob that if he worked for him another seven years then he would give him Rachael for his wife. So Jacob agreed. So Jacob now had two wives, although he really only wanted one- Rachael. Now the years passed and although Leah had already given ten sons to Jacob, Rachael had as yet, given him none.

Then the Lord looked upon Rachael and had compassion for her, and she conceived a son and named him Joseph. He was Jacob's eleventh son and also his favorite because he was born of Rachael.

I gave you this background about Joseph so you would better understand the rest of Joseph's story. It did not take long for Joseph's brothers to see how much their father favored Joseph. His father made him a very special coat of many colors, and when they saw the coat their father had made for Joseph, they hated Joseph from that day on.

It was during this time also that God began giving dreams to Joseph about his future. He showed him in two separate dreams that all of his brothers, and even his father would one day bow down to him. When he woke up, he told his brothers and his father about his dream and they were all astonished, but from that day on his brothers sought out how they might get rid of him secretly, so as not to incite their father's anger towards them.

That day soon came. Joseph was seventeen years old when this event occurred. Joseph's brothers were all out feeding their father's flock of sheep. Much time passed and they had not returned home, so Joseph's father sent him out to check on his brothers. When he finally found them they were not with the flock, but instead in a town called Dothan.

As Joseph approached, they saw him from far off and conspired together to kill him. They devised a plan to kill him and throw his body into a pit. They would then tell their father Jacob, that a wild beast had killed him. Reuben however, talked his brothers out of killing him, hoping that later he could come back to pull Joseph out of the pit and bring him back home safely.

Now his brothers were sitting near the pit and began eating a meal when they saw a caravan of merchants coming near. Judah talked them into selling Joseph as a slave to the travelers, thereby solving both problems. They would not have Joseph's blood on their hands and

Joseph would be gone to them forever. So that is what they did.

When they returned home, they told their father that Joseph was killed and eaten by a wild beast, and they brought his coat of many colors back to their father. Their father was so heart broken that he refused any comfort that his sons tried to give him. Meanwhile, Joseph was sold as a slave in Egypt to a man named Potiphar, and Captain of the guard. So Joseph was far away from his father and his mother who loved him dearly, and was a slave in a far off land to a foreign people.

In chapter thirty-nine of Genesis, it says that God was with Joseph, and made him successful in his master's house, and prospered everything that Joseph did (Genesis 39:2). Now the scripture reveals that Joseph had a special calling upon his life, yet so far, his life seemed to be filled with nothing but pain, suffering, and tears. Joseph had also been given the gift of prophetical dreams and the ability to interpret them from when he first experienced it as a child.

God showed him in a dream as a child, that he would be exalted to a position of great power and influence one day. His life thus far however, seemed to reflect anything but this, and the events that were soon to follow only served to magnify this fact.

So let us go on with Joseph's story. Joseph's master, Potiphar, saw very quickly that God was with him, and so he made Joseph overseer over all the affairs of his home (Genesis 39:1-6). Joseph was also a very handsome young man according to scripture (Genesis 39:6), and it did not take long for Potiphar's wife to begin to pursue Joseph, and make advances toward him.

After many failed attempts, and being continually rejected by Joseph, she became enraged at being spurned and made false accusations against him to her husband. He believed his wife's story, and promptly had Joseph thrown into the king's prison. Immediately, the guard in charge of the prison saw how God was with Joseph, and made Joseph head of all the prisoners, and gave him the authority to do as he wished there (Genesis 39:20-23).

Not long after, two men who served the Pharoah were placed in the prison where Joseph was, for offending the Pharoah, a baker and a butler, and the Captain of the guard put Joseph in charge of them also. One night, both the butler and the baker each had a dream on the same night that caused them to be greatly saddened when they awoke the next morning.

When Joseph saw their sad countenances, he inquired as to why. They both replied that they each had a troubling dream the night before, and were upset because they did not understand what their dreams meant. Joseph asked them to tell him their dreams from the night before, and so they did. Immediately Joseph explained to each of them what their dreams meant. One would be pardoned by the Pharoah, and one would be executed.

Three days later was Pharoah's birthday, and the Pharoah called the baker and the butler out of prison, and did to each one just as Joseph had foretold (Genesis 40:1-23). Joseph had only asked the butler that in return for his interpretation of his dream, that he would remember him when he was free, but the butler did not remember his kindness.

Two full years later, Pharoah had a dream in the night that woke him up. He then fell back asleep and had another dream that woke him up, and his spirit was troubled because he did not understand what his two dreams meant (Genesis 41:1-7). So Pharoah sent for his magicians to interpret his troubling dreams, but none of them could understand them. It was this precise moment that Joseph's destiny was manifested into his life...

The butler who had been in prison with Joseph, and later released as Joseph had foretold, remembered Joseph and his gift for interpreting dreams. It was now the time that he told Pharoah about Joseph's gift. So Pharoah sent for Joseph to be brought to him, and it was so. The Pharoah proceeded to tell Joseph of his troubling dreams from the night before, and asks him to interpret them for him because he has heard that Joseph has the ability to do this.

Joseph responds to Pharoah by saying this, "It is not for me; God will give Pharoah an answer for peace (Genesis 41:15). So Joseph interprets Pharoah's dreams, and the Pharoah is so impressed with his wisdom and discernment that this is his reply, "In as much as God has shown you all this, there is no one as discerning and as wise as you. You shall be over my house, and all my people shall be ruled according to your word; only in regard to my throne will I be greater than you. See, I have set you over all the land of Egypt" (Genesis 41:39-41).

Joseph, in this moment, begins to see his destiny unfold before his eyes. Then Pharoah took his signet ring off his hand and put it on Joseph's hand, and he clothed him in fine linen and put a gold chain around his neck. And he had him ride in the second Chariot which he had, and they cried out before him, "Bow the knee!", and so he st him over all the land of Egypt.

So now we begin to see the pieces falling into place for Joseph. The only thing missing from his dream from long ago was his brothers, and they were living in a land far away from where he was. That however, was all fixing to change. Joseph had told the Pharoah that the meaning of his two dreams meant that the next seven years would be ones of blessing and fruitfulness upon the land, and the seven years after that would be ones of great famine upon the land and all the lands around it.

Joseph advised Pharoah to stock up on all food supplies for the next seven years of prosperity, in order to be ready for the following seven years of famine. The Pharoah did as Joseph advised and Egypt's granaries were full. When the seven years of famine came, all the countries around Egypt were starving from the famine. They heard that Egypt had bread, so they all came to Joseph in Egypt to buy bread for their people. Now Jacob, Joseph's father instructed his sons to travel to Egypt to go and buy bread for their household so they would not starve.

However, Jacob did not send his youngest son Benjamin with them for fear that something would happen to him as did Joseph. Benjamin was born after Joseph was gone, so Joseph had no idea that he had a younger brother by his mother Rachael. Now Rachael had died while giving birth to Benjamin, so he was the only child left by Rachael that Jacob knew of, for he believed Joseph to be dead.

Now Joseph was Governor over all the land of Egypt, and it was he who sold the bread to all the people who came in need of it. When Joseph's brothers entered into Egypt, they came before Joseph and bowed down before him with their faces to the earth, just as Joseph dreamed many years past as foretold.

They also did not recognize Joseph, but he recognized them. He acted as a stranger to them and spoke roughly to them, asking them, "Where do you come from (Genesis 42:1-7)? They replied that they had come from the land of Canaan to buy bread.

Joseph had many emotions that he was feeling at that moment, but chose not to reveal them yet. He was interested in knowing where his brothers' hearts were, so he chose to put them through a test. It was in this test that Joseph discovered that he had a younger brother named Benjamin, and that his brothers carried immense remorse, guilt, and shame over what they had done to Joseph, and of the incurable grief it had brought to their father over the loss of Joseph.

After a series of events, Joseph finally revealed himself to his brothers and they were reunited to one another. It was a very emotional event (Genesis 42: 41-45). His brothers returned to Canaan to get their father Jacob and their brother Benjamin, and they returned to Egypt where Joseph was waiting. It was a very happy family reunion at long last!

Joseph was finally reunited with his father Jacob who had believed him to be dead all these years, and it was truly a very happy ending for their family.

One very important statement that Joseph says to his brothers when he revealed himself to them gives great insight as to WHY their story ended so well, and it was this, "I am Joseph, the one you sold into Egypt! And now, do not be distressed, and do not be angry with yourselves for selling me here. It was to save lives that God sent me ahead of you. For two years now there has been a famine in the land, and for the next five years there will be no plowing or reaping. But God sent me ahead of you to preserve you for a remnant on earth and to save your lives by a great deliverance. So then, it was not you, but God" (Genesis 45: 1-8).

This conversation reveals something extremely important...Joseph's perspective. Joseph had the CHOICE as to how he was going to look at, and feel about his situation and his past. There are many ways that Joseph could have looked at his past and all the wrong that had been done to him by his own family.

He could have chosen to hate his brothers, and not forgive them. He could have chosen to retaliate, and put them all into prison to suffer as he had, but instead, Joseph CHOSE to see God's plan in it all, and that it was all for a greater purpose for Joseph, his family, and Israel's survival as a people.

You see, we all experience bad things in our lives, some just and some unjust, but how we choose to look at it and feel about it is **ALWAYS OUR CHOICE**, and this **ONE CHOICE** will direct the course of our future. **WE MUST UNDERSTAND**

THIS if we are ever to have a good future ahead of us. People WILL hurt us. They WILL let us down. They may even abandon us, but God NEVER WILL.

Chapter Four: A Man Named Paul

Now I am going to tell you a story about a man named Paul, but we are going to go back to a time when he had a different name. A time when he was called Saul of Tarsus. Saul of Tarsus was both a Roman citizen and a Jewish Pharisee of the highest order. He lived during the time of Jesus, yet had never personally met him.

After Jesus' death and resurrection however, he was on a full-fledged mission to capture, imprison, torture, and kill every person known to be one of Jesus' disciples, or followers. He had the complete support and backing of both the Jewish leadership and the Roman government.

He was highly respected by both the Jewish Pharisees and Sanhedrin, and the Roman officials. He was also greatly feared and dreaded by every follower of Jesus because Saul's goal was to hunt down and kill every single Christian until there was not one left alive. Saul viewed Christians as enemies to God and to the Jewish faith, and was on a rampage to hunt them down like criminals and make examples out of them all...but God had other plans.

Saul was on a mission which he believed was possibly the most important mission of his life. He was convinced that what he was doing was God's will. But Saul could not have been more wrong. He had just left the stoning and murder of a disciple of Jesus, named Stephen, to which he gave his wholehearted approval (Acts 7: 57-60).

After this event, Saul was on his way to Damascus with letters from the Jewish synagogue, to arrest and imprison all who proclaimed to be followers of Jesus, and to bring them to Jerusalem to face trial (Acts 8: 1,2). Saul had a great zeal for the Lord, but he lacked knowledge. Now God was going to change that.

So Saul was traveling with a regiment of Roman soldiers on the road to Damascus when suddenly, a great light fell from Heaven, shone all around him, and a clap of thunder cracked the sky. It knocked Saul off his horse to the ground, and he heard a voice from Heaven say, "Saul, Saul, why are you persecuting me?", and Saul replied, "Who are you Lord?". Then the Lord said, "I am Jesus whom you are persecuting. It is hard for you to kick against the goads" (Acts 5: 1-5).

In one moment... EVERYTHING changed! Saul's life had now changed forever. Just like Saul, many times, we might believe we are doing the right thing, when in fact, it is not. The bible states,

"There is a way which SEEMS right to a man, but in the end is DEATH, (Proverbs 14: 12).

One encounter with Jesus, as we have seen, can change everything. No matter WHAT we have done in our past, God CAN, and IS WILLING to forgive us. We need only to ask. The bible says that if we CONFESS OUR SIN, that God is faithful and just to FORGIVE US OUR SIN (1 John 1:8-9). It also says that if we CONFESS WITH OUR MOUTH that Jesus is Lord, and BELIEVE IN OUR HEART that God raised Him from the dead, then we SHALL BE SAVED, (Romans 10: 9-10).

God forgave Saul for his prior sins when he repented and received Christ, but he still had a past that brought him great shame, grief, and torment. He could not undo the terrible things he had done, but he COULD change, and he did, as we can clearly see in the rest of his story.

God then changed Saul's name to Paul. This was the beginning of Paul being set free from the chains that bound his heart to his past. Everyone knew who Paul was, and all of the harm he had done to the followers of Jesus. Paul's sins were so grievous that the Jewish leaders, the Roman government, and many of the Jews were hunting him down to take his life, and make an example out of him.

It was the followers of Jesus that actually took Paul in and hid him until they could get him safely out of the city of Damascus. It would take time for Paul to be able to leave behind the pain of his past. Time for Paul to become confident in his new identity, and God gave him that.

After Paul presented himself before the Apostles of Jesus to let them see for themselves, that his conversion was genuine, he fled to the desert, where he spent the following 17 years alone with God. Through the power of God's grace and mercy, and revelations given to him by the Holy Spirit, Paul began to learn truths that would change the church of Christ forever.

There are some important lessons that we can learn from Paul's story, one of them being that we **MUST MAKE PEACE WITH OUR PAST** if we want to move forward with our life. As the Lord once told me, it comes to mind again, "You **CANNOT** go **TWO DIRECTIONS** at the same time". In other words, you cannot move forward in your life while living in your past...It is literally impossible!

Paul went on to become, as many people believe, the greatest Apostle of all time, but not until **HE FORGAVE HIMSELF** for his past actions and sins he had committed. He had to be free of his own guilt and shame before he could do all that God had given him to do. It had to be settled once and for all, and it took the hand of God to accomplish this.

The wonderful news is that God can do this for ANY PERSON that is WILLING to allow Him to do it for them, and that includes you and me. If you have a past that is haunting you day after day; a past that will not let you go, then you are in the right place. Maybe God has you here, right now, for such a time as this. If you want freedom from the pain, the shame, the guilt, then you can have that today.

Pray with me now...

"Father, I come to you right now, asking for your forgiveness. I have sinned against you, against Heaven, and against all those that I have hurt and wronged. I am sorry for all of my sins and I want to change. I want to be free from my past, and to become who you created me to be. I believe that Jesus Christ is the Messiah and Savior of the world. I believe that He came to this world and lived as a man, that He died on the cross for my sins, was buried and rose again on the third day. Because He lives, I will live also with Him in Heaven one day. Jesus, please forgive my sins, come into my heart and my life, and be my Lord and Savior from this day forward. I give my life to you. It is YOURS."

Now, if you have prayed this prayer today, then you are a NEW CREATION, born anew of the Spirit of God, and indwelt by His Holy Spirit who will NEVER LEAVE YOU OR FORSAKE YOU... the old is PAST AWAY! Your next step is to get a bible and start reading His word. Then, find a church to attend and tell others of your decision to follow Christ, and in obedience to His word, be baptized in water and ask Him for the baptism of the Holy Spirit. This is the gift to all believers in Christ. Welcome to the family of God, and the greatest adventure you will ever know!

Now, I will share one more story with you... my own.

Chapter Five: My Story

My name is Karen Stines- Watt- Dowling, and I am 63 years old. I have six amazing grown children and a flock of beautiful grandchildren! I am **TRULY BLESSED!** I am a writer, a painter, a musician, a student in college, a lover of nature and traveling, and foremost, I am a child of God, Yahweh, and a bond-servant of Jesus Christ. I am also a recovering addict from a 37 year addiction and struggle.

Getting free from active addiction was a life long struggle for me. I am 63 years old and have spent 37 of those years in active addiction. In my past I have been a user of methamphetamine, cocaine, crack, hydrocodone, oxycontin, zanex, acid, mushrooms, marajuana, and alcohol. I was also an IV user. I tell you this because I want you to understand **HOW EXTENSIVE** my addiction was, and I had come to believe that I would never find freedom from it's terrible grip on my life.

Addiction is a **HORRIBLE PRISON**. One with bars that cannot be seen with the physical eyes, but **JUST AS REAL** as a prison with bars that you **CAN** see.

Let me go back some years to when it all began for me. I was a teenager growing up in the 60's and 70's in a middle-class family with two parents. My family had some problems just as MANY families do, but not bad enough for me to blame my parents for my using. But I did for some years when I was younger.

I began using because I wanted to. Because my friends were, and because it was fun… at first. The bible states that, "Sin is pleasurable, FOR A SEASON!" (Hebrews 11: 25-26). But that season soon ends and by then you are hooked!

I was 17 years old, fresh out of high school, and began using along with my "high school sweetheart". We were using methamphetamine by the needle. That summer, I became pregnant. We wanted to keep our baby, but knew that our lifestyle as full-fledged drug addicts was no life for a child to be brought up in. So reluctantly, we decided to give our child the gift that we could not give him, a wonderful life and a bright future through adoption. I will never forget holding my beautiful son in my arms, and knowing I would have to let him go, never to see him again. It was more than I could bear! My heart was broken in a way I had never known. I did it for him, but it was a pain that I would carry in my heart for many years to come.

After I gave birth to my first child, my first love and high school sweetheart informed me that while I was gone having the baby, his parents had sold their home and was moving to Arizona. He was given an ultimatum... either leave with his family or they would disinherit him. He came from a family that was fairly wealthy. Long story short, he reluctantly left with them. In one moment I had lost my beautiful child and my first love.

My heart so broken that I could not bear it. After that, I did not care about anything, and I dove head first as deep as I could go into a world of constant drug use to escape the pain of my reality. The next three years were just a blur for me, as I cared about nothing other than staying high. I got involved with all the wrong people, serious people, dangerous people. Then came the news. I was pregnant again.

The ONLY thing I knew for sure was that I COULD NOT lose another child because of addiction. So I went into a drug rehab and spent the next four months in treatment. When it was time to have my baby I left the rehab and moved in with my parents, who were more than happy to help me raise my son.

About three months after my son was born I met the man that would be my future husband, and father of my next four children. It was one month after we met, and my birthday. He gave me my first bible. Neither one of us were Christians, or even went to church, but that was what he gave me- a bible!

I never stopped being amazed by that gift because three years later we both gave our hearts to the Lord and that was my very first bible that I began to learn about God from when we began attending church. It was so special to me because this gift that I received three years prior to being born again, told me that GOD KNEW before we did that this day would come.

During those difficult times that were to come, the Lord became my strength, my comforter, my teacher, and my refuge. I learned to depend on Him, to trust in Him, and to look to Him for all my needs. Life was not perfect, but it was manageable.

The, ten years into our marriage, the most destructive, terrifying force I had ever encountered came back into our life... drugs. The most devastating part of it all was that I never saw it coming. For our marriage and our beautiful family, it was the beginning of the end.

My husband had been out of work for several months and we had just had our youngest daughter. She was two months old. I remember the day it happened like it was yesterday. My husband had been "MIA" for almost two weeks and although he had never done it before, I was starting to think that maybe he was cheating on me. It could not have been further from the truth!

The truth actually turned out to be far worse. He was using methamphetamine.

I was just finishing up a bible study at our home when I got the call. It was him, telling me that he wanted to talk, and that he was on his way to our house. When he arrived, I honestly did not know what to expect, so I just sat there and let him talk.

He told me that he suspected that I thought he was cheating on me, but he wasn't. He confessed that he had been doing speed, and not just any speed, the "good stuff". The stuff that hadn't been around since the seventies, and it was now 1994.

I just remember feeling frozen. I did not know what to say. In the past ten years of our life, I had never once thought about that stuff. I had left it behind for good. Or so I thought. But I was so wrong. In the next moment I remember him saying that he had some on him and asked if I wanted to do some.

Before I even knew what I was saying, I said "yes". I don't know why. I think that maybe it was because I felt like it would bridge the space that had been between us for the past couple of months. But I said it. I said yes.

In that one moment everything in our lives would change forever. We had opened up the famous "Pandora's Box", when once opened, cannot be shut. I spent the rest of the night crying my eyes out for the choice I had made, and could not undo.

Fast forward ten years ahead. The year was 2004. My husband and I of 21 years got a divorce, and our innocent children were all dragged through the whole traumatic ordeal. Their world was shattered, as was ours. At this particular time, we both had stopped doing speed BUT, we had taken on new addictions, marijuana, pills, alcohol, crack, and cocaine.

It was one never-ending nightmare for all of us. Another HUGE factor that had happened over the past 10 years, was that my heart had become consumed with hatred and blame towards my husband, and deep anger towards God.

Many horrible things continued to happen and eventually I ended up in jail and my three youngest children were in the hands of Child Protective Services. After serving three months in jail I was given probation, and through lots of hard work, determination, and staying clean, I got my children back and gained full custody of them. That was one of the happiest moments of my life.

I was heavily involved in Narcotics Anonymous, was newly remarried to another member of N.A. that had 13 years clean. I landed a great job of managing a children's hair shop, making very good money, and my three youngest children, who were now becoming teenagers, were living with me and my new husband. But I was a different person now then I was in my first marriage. I was very independent, angry with men, and no active relationship with God other than going to church on Sundays. I was no longer willing to take abuse, in ANY FORM from a man.

I was still trapped in my past, still asking God WHY He had let this happen to me and my first beautiful family... but the answers never came. Pretty soon the fighting started between my new husband and me, and it quickly spiraled into physical fights. It was then that I began using drugs again. Crack, pills, alcohol. Basically anything I could get my hands on, and I had lots of money to fund my addiction with.

Within a year my life fell apart once again I was getting another divorce, and moving out with my three girls. I spent the next five years battling my addictions with no success. Then one fateful day, speed came back into my life. I owned my own house, was manager of a hair shop, yet miserable. I soon lost my dream job, and soon after my dream house went too. All because of my addiction. I went into a severe depression, was smoking crack all day long, drinking a fifth of whiskey a day, smoking unlimited amounts of marijuana, and taking 8 hydrocodones a day.

      The first day I began using speed again, I had stayed up for three days, when I realized that I had not touched any of my other addictions for those three days. I decided that day that maybe speed was not so bad after all because it had freed me from all of my other addictions in one moment.

In my eyes, it was my savior, but I was so wrong! In reality, all I did was trade one addiction for another once again, but I could not see that then. So I made four rules for myself that day regarding my use of speed, that I committed myself to. This would ensure my ability to "use successfully" in my mind.

Fast forward another ten years. Now it was the year 2023- January. I was working a job for about a year and a half, that I loved. I well loved by all of my co-workers and my residents that I served. I excelled at my job. I had been attending college online for a year and a half, making straight "A"s. I had my own apartment and my two adult children living with me. I paid all my bills

EXCEPT that I had let all of my car stickers go out of date, and had stopped paying my car insurance.

I had even attempting re-establishing my relationship with the Lord again, BUT I was still using speed. To my knowledge, no one other than my immediate family had a clue that I was an addict. The thinking in my mind was that I had learned the secret of being a "successful user", and that I had everything under control... until, that one fateful day in January 2023, when me and my daughter were on our way back into town from a Christmas trip we had taken out of town.

We were about 100 miles from getting back home and I got pulled over. That was the moment when my whole world, and all of my illusions came crashing down. Thirty minutes later I was being hauled off to jail for having illegal substances in my car, and everything regarding my car was out of date. My daughter, who was extremely mentally impaired at the time, was made to drive my car the last 100 miles to our home. I was devastated!

Everything I had led myself to believe about "using successfully" went out the window in one fateful moment. For the first time, I had to face the awful truth... that there is **NO SUCH THING AS SUCCESSFUL USING!** There are only **THREE ROADS** that using drugs leads to in the end... jails, institutions, and death!

I don't know a lot of things, but one thing I DO KNOW, is WHERE TO GO when my life is falling apart. Jesus. A day later I was bonded out of jail by my ex-husband, and he drove the 100 miles to come pick me up and bring me back home in time to resume my job without anyone there knowing what had happened.

He never condemned me or chastised me in any way. All he did was show me the love, mercy, and compassion that God shows us. I went back to work the next day and never said a word about what had happened. One thing though that I knew for sure was that my life HAD to change!

Fast forward one year. Life is much better now, and I will tell you why. I am now clean and sober, but it did not come by magic. I had to take a long, hard look at myself, and my life. I was doing okay before... I THOUGHT, however, I was trying to do it alone. I was still living with the same unresolved hurts and anger that I had been carrying around for twenty years. That is a LONG time to stay stuck! I had not truly forgiven myself, my ex-husband, but especially God.

I can tell you this. I still do not have the answers as to WHY things happened as they did, but I DO KNOW THIS... not once did God EVER LEAVE ME. I left him. He was there every step of the way. I just could not see it then, but I do now.

One thing He did tell me that changed my life was this- He said, "Karen, you CANNOT go TWO DIRECTIONS at the SAME TIME. It is impossible". I knew at that moment what He meant. What He meant was this: you CANNOT go forward until you LET GO of the past!

So finally, I did.

Chapter Six: Final Thoughts

My final words to you are this: **FORGIVE.**

Not if they deserve it, or ask for it, or even want it.

Forgiveness is for **YOU**. You are the one that stays

stuck in the prison of hate. Sometimes it is guilt,

or shame, or fear, or even pride. None of it will

help you or set you free to live a life worth living. You HAVE to let it go. It will be the most important and life-changing decision you will ever make.

DON"T let pride stand in the way of your freedom. Pride never did anything for anyone except keep them stuck! Your life and your freedom are waiting for you. All you have to do is LET GO and TRUST GOD. He will do the rest. Leave the past where it belongs... in the past.

"Forgetting what lies behind, and reaching forward to what lies ahead, I press on towards the goal for the prize of the upward call of God in Christ Jesus" (Philippians 3: 13-14, NASB, (1995)).

References:

- Job 1: 1-7, 13-19, 20-22
- Job2: 1-10
- Job 42: 5, 12-15
- Genesis 29: 20, 39: 1-6, 20-23, 40: 1-23, 41:1-7, 15, 39-41
- Genesis 42:1-7, 41-45
- Genesis 45: 1-8
- Acts 7: 57-60
- Acts 8:1-2
- Acts 9:1-5
- Proverbs 14:12
- 1 John 1: 8-9

- **Romans 10: 9-10**

- **Hebrews 11: 25-26**

- **Philippians 3: 13-14**

Made in the USA
Columbia, SC
24 November 2024